COVERED BRIDGES

IN WEST VIRGINIA

Stephen J. Shaluta, Jr.

QUARRIER PRESS
Charleston, West Virginia

Quarrier Press
Charleston, WV

10 9 8 7 6 5 4 3 2 1

Printed in China

Library of Congress Number : 2003096899

ISBN : 1-891852-32-9

Book Design:
Colleen Anderson/Mother Wit Writing and Design

Cover photo of Fletcher Creek Covered Bridge by author

Distributed by:
Pictorial Histories Distribution
1125 Central Avenue
Charleston, WV 25302
www.wvbookco.com

COVERED BRIDGES
IN WEST VIRGINIA

In 1983, while working in a career as a railroad engineer—and as an amateur photographer—I was approached by a publisher to work on a photographic book on the covered bridges of West Virginia. My interest in photography had begun in August of 1978—less than five years earlier—so having a publisher notice my photography was quite flattering.

One major hurdle in taking on this project was that I knew absolutely nothing about covered bridges. One advantage I had was that Myrtle Auvil, author of *Covered Bridges of West Virginia Past and Present*, lived in my hometown of Grafton, WV.

I began the project with excitement, reading Myrtle's book, traveling the state and shooting (what I thought at the time was) extreme amounts of film. I kept accurate records on the location and directions to each bridge and also recorded details of photographic information and lighting conditions. Within a year I had photographed the seventeen remaining covered bridges in West Virginia, and in 1985 the book *West Virginia Covered Bridges* was released. In 1992 some of the same photos from this book were used in Stan Cohen's book, *West Virginia Covered Bridges: A Pictorial Heritage*.

In 2002 I was approached by Quarrier Press to do another photographic book on West Virginia covered bridges… ahh a second chance! Over the years my photographic abilities have greatly improved, but more importantly my appreciation of the history and beauty of covered bridges has matured. Over the last twenty years I have photographed and re-photographed West Virginia's covered bridges. I've traveled to neighboring states to photograph their covered bridges, and I never miss the opportunity to take photos of covered bridges while on assignment or vacation.

In 1983 seventeen covered bridges remained standing in West Virginia. I am happy to report that twenty years later seventeen covered bridges still remain standing, although the Philippi Covered Bridge nearly burned to the ground in February 1989. The West Virginia Department of Transportation has recently renovated the fourteen bridges that remain on the state highway system (three are on private property).

Eight of the seventeen bridges are completely closed to vehicular traffic, but that leaves nine that are traveled daily by a variety of vehicles. Most of these structures are located on sparsely traveled rural roads, with one major exception. The covered bridge at Philippi, located on US Route 250, is exposed to a large amount of traffic each day, although a "truck route" bridge was recently built nearby.

West Virginia covered bridges are located generally in three clusters. The largest cluster is in the north central region of the state, where nine structures reside within seven counties. Three bridges located within two western counties make up the second cluster. In the final cluster, five bridges are located within three bordering counties in the southeastern area of the state.

At one time, fifty-eight documented covered bridges stood throughout West Virginia, although it is thought that one hundred or more were built at various times. One I distinctly remember is the covered bridge across the Cheat River on US Route 50 in Preston County. As a child our family would often go on Sunday drives along Route 50 east of Grafton, WV. We sometimes stopped at a picnic area located at the entrance to the Cheat River Covered Bridge. This bridge burned to the ground in 1964, leaving an empty hole in my memory of the area. To this day, as I travel this road working on photography assignments I can still see the image of this bridge in my mind.

Steve Shaluta

COVERED BRIDGES IN WEST VIRGINIA

Barrackville Covered Bridge .... Marion County

Carrollton Covered Bridge .... Barbour County

Center Point Covered Bridge .... Doddridge County

Dents Run Covered Bridge .... Monongalia County

Fish Creek Covered Bridge .... Wetzel County

Fletcher or Ten Mile Creek Covered Bridge .... Harrison County

Herns Mill or Milligan Creek Covered Bridge .... Greenbrier County

Hokes Mill or Second Creek Covered Bridge .... Greenbrier County

Indian Creek Covered Bridge .... Monroe County

Lily Dale or Laurel Creek Covered Bridge .... Monroe County

Locust Creek Covered Bridge .... Pocahontas County

Milton or Mud River Covered Bridge .... Cabell County

Philippi Covered Bridge .... Barbour County

Sandy Creek or Sarvis Fork Covered Bridge .... Jackson County

Simpson Creek or Hollens Mill Covered Bridge .... Harrison County

Staats Mill Covered Bridge .... Jackson County

Walkersville Covered Bridge .... Lewis County

Barrackville

BARRACKVILLE

Lemuel Chenoweth, a covered bridge builder and contractor from Beverly, built the Barrackville covered bridge in 1853. It is a multiple kingpost truss with a Burr arch, 148 feet in length and 20 feet wide. The bridge was completely restored in 1999.

Directions: The covered bridge is located on Marion County Route 21 in Barrackville.

Barrackville

Carrollton

CARROLLTON

The second longest and third oldest covered bridge in West Virginia, the Carrollton covered bridge was built in 1856, by contractors Daniel and Emmett J. O'Brien of Beverly. About 140 feet in length and 16 feet in width, this bridge is one of three examples in West Virginia of the patented Burr Arch truss structure. The bridge was upgraded in the early 1960s, but the covering and the sides of the old bridge were left intact. It was completely restored in 2003.

Directions: From the junction of US Routes 119 and 250 in Philippi, take Route 119 south 6 miles to CR 36 (Carrollton Road). Turn left and drive .7 miles directly to the bridge over the Buckhannon River.

CENTER POINT

The only covered bridge in Doddridge County, the Center Point Bridge was built sometime between 1888-90. T.W. Ancell and E. Underwood built the abutments; John Ash and S.H. Smith built the superstructure. It is located on private land over Talkington Fork of McElroy Creek, and is 42.1 feet in length and 12.6 feet wide. It was completely restored in 2004.

Directions: From US Route 50 west of Salem, take secondary Route 23. Drive 10.2 miles to Pike Fork Road 10. When you get to a small right turn here, please stop. The bridge is within easy sight of the public road, but is on private property.

DENTS RUN

Built sometime after 1889, Dents Run is the only covered bridge remaining in Monongalia County. W.Y. Loar built the abutments and William and Joseph Mercer built the superstructure. It is 40 feet in length and 12 feet wide.

Directions: From I-79, take Westover exit 152. Turn south on US Route 19 and drive 3.2 miles to Sugar Grove Road. Turn right and drive .7 miles watching carefully on the left for a gravel road. Turn left at the gravel road and drive .1 mile directly to the bridge.

Dents Run

FISH CREEK

Accurate history of the construction of Fish Creek Bridge is unknown, but it is thought to have been built about 1880-81 by relatives of C.W. Critchfield. The bridge is 36 feet long and 13 feet wide. It was completely restored in 2000.

Directions: Fish Creek covered bridge is located at the junction of US Route 250 and CR 13 near the town of Hundred, in Wetzel County.

Fish Creek

FLETCHER BRIDGE
BRIDGE NO. 4368
BUILT CIRCA 1891
REHABILITATED 2002

Fletcher or Ten Mile Creek

FLETCHER *or* TEN MILE CREEK

Built in 1891, L.E. Sturm built the abutments and Soloman Swiger built the Kingpost truss superstructure. It is 58 feet in length and 12 feet wide. It was completely restored in 2002.

Directions: Travel US Route 50 west of Clarksburg, and take Marshville exit 5. Drive 1.6 miles to this bridge located over the right-hand fork of Ten Mile Creek.

Herns Mill

HERNS MILL or MILLIGAN CREEK

Unfortunately the names of the builders have been lost, but it is believed this bridge was built sometime between 1879 and 1884. It was built using a variation of the Queenpost truss design and is 54 feet in length and 10.5 feet wide. At one time this bridge provided access to the S.S. Hern Mill. It was completely restored in 2000.

Directions: From the junction of US Routes 219 and 60 in downtown Lewisburg, take US Route 60 west 3.5 miles to Bungers Mill Road 60/11. Turn left and drive .2 miles to Herns Mill Road 40 and turn left again. Drive 1 mile directly to Herns Mill Bridge over Milligan Creek.

Herns Mill or Milligan Creek

Herns Mill or Milligan Creek

HOKES MILL *or* SECOND CREEK

The completion of this bridge is estimated to have been between 1897 and 1899. B.F. Mann, R.A. McDowell and Austin B. Erwin were appointed by the county commission to have the bridge constructed for $700. Utilizing a modified Long truss, the bridge is more than 81 feet long and 12 feet wide. It was completely restored in 2002.

Directions: From the junction of US Routes 219 and 60 in downtown Lewisburg, take US 219 south 4.9 miles to River Road CR 48. This road is located on the south end of the Greenbrier River Bridge in Ronceverte. Turn right and drive 5 miles directly to the bridge located over Second Creek on your left.

Hokes Mill or Second Creek

Indian Creek

INDIAN CREEK

Oscar and Ray Weikel, then only 16 and 18 years old, built this bridge near Union in 1898–99. Utilizing a modified Howe truss, the bridge is about 49 feet in length and 12 feet wide and cost about $400. Although the bridge was abandoned in the late 1920s or early 1930s, the Monroe County Historical Society leased it in 1965. A brother of the original builders was hired to strengthen it. It was completely restored in 2000.

Directions: Start on US Route 219 in Union, and drive south on US 219 about 5 miles directly to the bridge on the west side.

Indian Creek

Lily Dale

LILY DALE *or* LAUREL CREEK

This bridge was built in about 1911. Lewis Miller constructed the stone abutments and Charles Robert Arnott built the superstructure. At 25 feet in length and 13 feet wide, it is the smallest covered bridge in the state. It was completely restored in the late 1990s.

Directions: From US Route 219 in Union, drive south on US 219 3.2 miles to Lily Dale Road 219/7 at Salt Sulphur Springs. Turn right and drive down Lily Dale Road for 3 miles where the road forks. Take the right fork, Laurel Creek Road 219/11, and continue for 1.4 miles directly to the bridge over Laurel Creek.

Locust Creek

LOCUST CREEK

Built in 1888 by R.N. Bruce, this bridge is 113 feet in length and was built in accordance with the double Warren truss system, near the Josiah Beard Mill. Records indicate that a bridge was located on this site as early as 1822, but it is not known if it was covered. Locust Creek Bridge was completely restored in 2002.

Directions: From Hillsboro, drive south on US 219 to Locust Creek Road, CR 20. Turn left and drive 3.3 miles to a stop sign, turn right and the bridge is located approximately 150 feet ahead.

Locust Creek

HISTORIC
MILTON COVERED
BRIDGE

Milton or Mud River

MILTON *or* MUD RIVER

Originally built on East Mud River Road in 1875-76, the Milton covered bridge was moved to the Cabell County Fair Grounds in 1997. This bridge is sometimes confused with a separate earlier covered bridge built nearby in 1834 and replaced in 1955. Supported by a modified Howe truss, the bridge is 108 feet in length and 14 feet wide. It was totally restored in 2001.

Directions: From I-64, east of Huntington take exit 28 (Milton) and turn toward Milton, drive .3 miles to US Route 60. Turn right onto US Route 60 West and drive .4 miles to the first stoplight. Turn left onto Fair Ground Road and drive .7 miles to One Pumpkin Way. The Milton covered bridge is located on your left.

Milton or Mud River

Philippi

PHILIPPI

Also known as the Lemuel Chenoweth Bridge after its builder, the Philippi covered bridge was constructed at a cost of about $12,180 in 1852. Lemuel and Eli Chenoweth of Beverly built the superstructure and Emmett J. O'Brien was the masonry contractor. The bridge is 285 feet long. It nearly burned to the ground in February 1989, and was completely restored and opened to traffic in the summer of 1991.

The span was built to facilitate use of the Beverly and Fairmont Road, which had been built in turn to stimulate use of the Staunton-Parkersburg Turnpike. One of six two-lane covered bridges remaining in the United States, it is the only one that still serves federal highway traffic – US Route 250. This bridge is believed to have escaped destruction during the Civil War because Union troops secured it early in the war. Used by both Northern and Southern troops, it is sometimes recognized as the site of the first land battle of the Civil War.

Directions: Located at the junction of US Routes 119 and 250 in Philippi.

Philippi

Sandy Creek or Sarvis Fork

SANDY CREEK *or* SARVIS FORK

Spanning the river that bears its name, Sandy Creek, this bridge is more than 101 feet in length and 11 feet wide. Using a modified Long system, George W. Staats originally built it over the John Carnahan Fork in 1889 for a cost of $64. In 1924 it was dismantled and rebuilt over the Left Fork of Big Sandy Creek, by C.R. Kent, R.R. Hardesty and E.R. Duke. The bridge was restored in 2000.

Directions: From downtown Ripley, start at the junction of US Route 33 and secondary Route 21. Drive Route 21 north for 10.9 miles to Sarvis Fork Road 21/15. Turn right and drive .2 miles directly to the bridge.

Simpson Creek

SIMPSON CREEK *or* HOLLENS MILL

Built in 1881 by Asa Hugill, the Simpson Creek covered bridge is a multiple Kingpost truss design and is 75 feet in length and 14 feet wide. In 1889 it was washed away by a flood and rebuilt in its current location .5 mile downstream. It was completely restored in 2002.

Directions: From I-79, take the Meadowbrook Road exit 121. Turn toward Meadowbrook Mall on secondary Route 24 and drive approximately .4 miles directly to the bridge on the left.

Staats Mill

STAATS MILL

Built in 1887 by H.T. Hartley, this bridge spanned the Tug Fork of Big Mill Creek at Staats Mill, about 9 miles southeast of Ripley. Hartley used the patented Long truss system to construct the 97 foot long and 11 foot wide span. The bridge was originally built in the area settled by Abraham and Ann King Staats, whose grandson Issac built Staats Mill. The bridge was moved in 1983 to its present location at Cedar Lakes State FFA-FHA camp near Ripley. It now serves as a walking bridge and its maintenance is the responsibility of the Cedar Lake Conference Center.

Directions: From downtown Ripley at the junction of US Route 33 and CR 21, take CR 21 south for .9 miles to a small sign on the right, which says "Cedar Lakes Road". Turn left and drive 1.7 miles to Cedar Lakes. The bridge sits over a pond inside the camp.

Walkersville

WALKERSVILLE

The Walkersville covered bridge is about 39 feet long and 12 feet wide. Built of Queenpost truss design, this bridge was built across the right fork of West Fork River in 1903 by John G. Sprigg. It was completely restored in 2003.

Directions: From I-79 south of Weston, take Roanoke exit 91. Drive south on US Route 19 for 13 miles to Big Run Road 19/17 just south of Walkersville. Turn right and the bridge will be within sight.

Walkersville

Stephen J. Shaluta, Jr.

In 1985, after nearly 15 years working as a locomotive engineer in my hometown of Grafton, WV, I resigned to become a full time photographer. This is a decision I have never regretted. My primary photography job is as a staff photographer for the West Virginia Division of Tourism, but I also have a successful freelance career.

For more than 20 years I have accumulated a long list of publication credits, through both my Tourism position and my freelance career. These credits include over 300 magazine covers, over 45 calendar covers, and three books. My photographs have also been published in newspapers, magazines, brochures, billboards and books used for editorial and advertising purposes. In recent years the exposure from my website has created an interest for framed and unframed enlarged prints of my photography.

Photography is my passion — my life. Even after nearly 17 years as a professional photographer the joy and excitement is still there. I have recently made the transition and embraced the new and exciting world of digital photography. With more editing control and printing capabilities I can see no limits to my creativity.

I hope you enjoy viewing the photography in this book as much as I have enjoyed shooting it. To see more of my photography and to order prints, please visit my website at **www.steveshaluta.com**.

COVERED BRIDGES IN WEST VIRGINIA